# THE HISTORY OF PHOTOGRAPHY IN PEN & INK
(abridged study guide)

*ILLUSTRATIONS*
*by*
**CHARLES WOODARD**

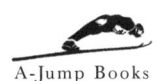

Athanasius Kircher
*Large Portable Camera Obscura.*
Engraving, 1646

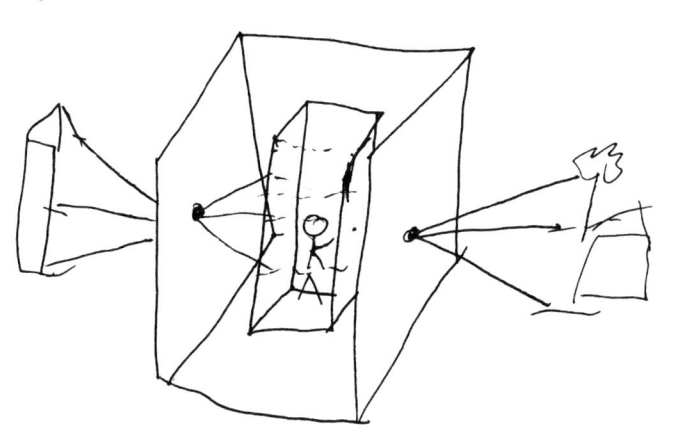

Louis Jacques Mande Daguerre
*Boulevard du Temple, Paris.*
Daguerreotype, c. 1838

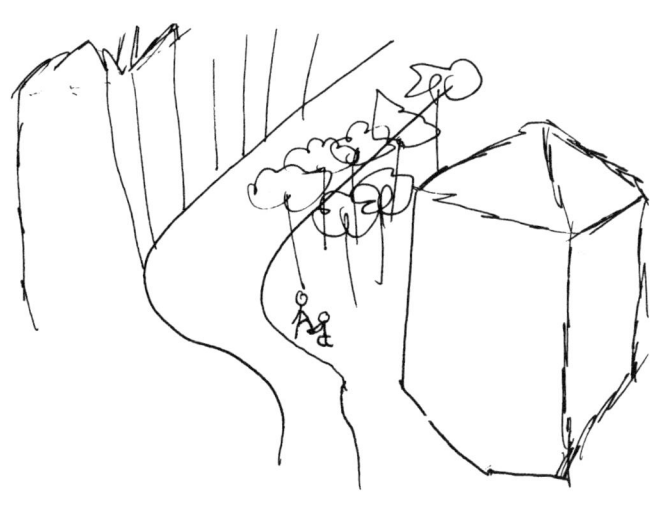

William Henry Fox Talbot
*Lacock Abbey.*
Salted paper print from paper negative, 1839

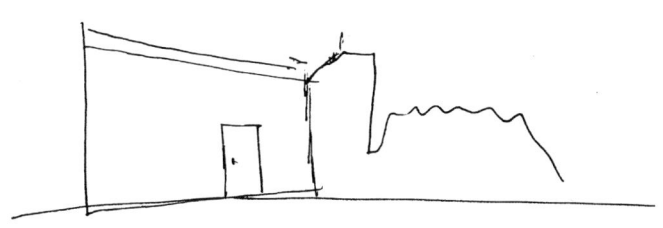

Hippolyte Bayard
*Self-Portrait as a Drowned Man.*
Direct paper positive, 1840

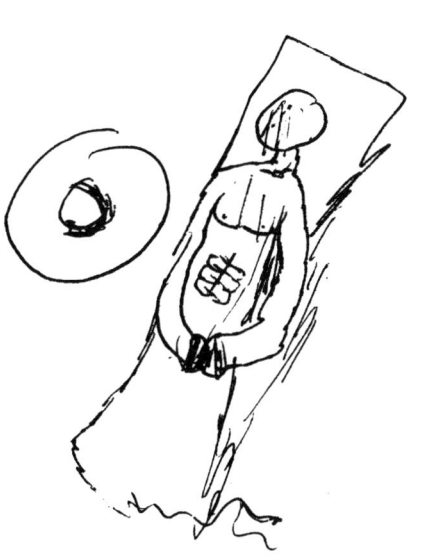

Albert Sands Southworth
*Self-Portrait.*
Daguerreotype, 1848

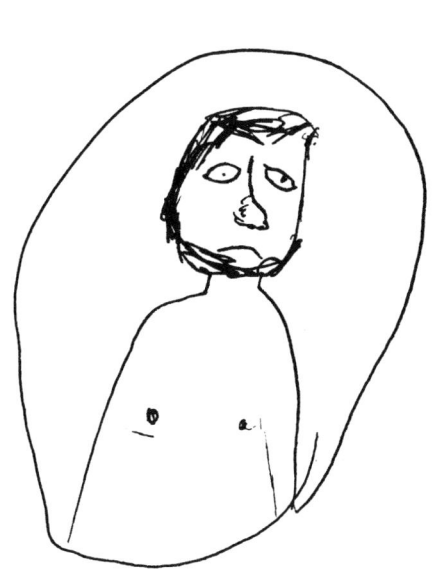

Mathew Brady
*John Calhoun.*
Daguerreotype, 1849 or 1850

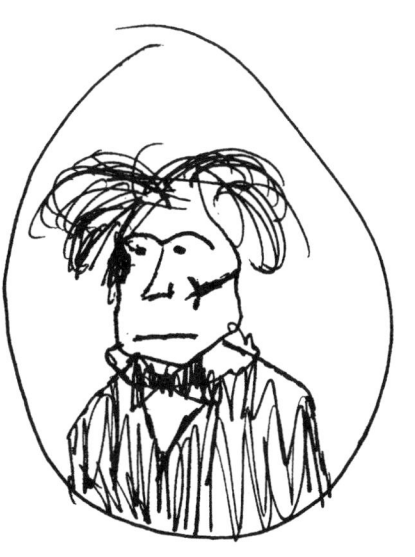

Nadar
*Charles Baudelaire.*
Salted paper print from wet-plate negative, 1855

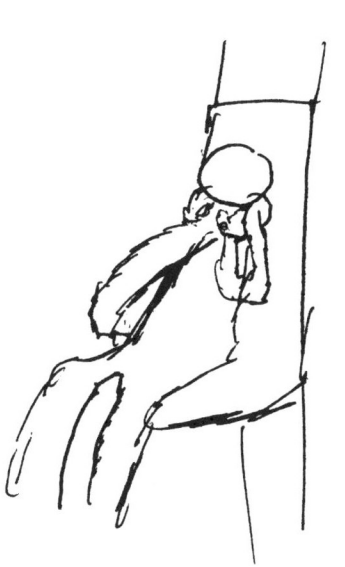

Dr. Hugh Diamond
*Religious Melancholy and Convalescence.*
Lithograph, 1856

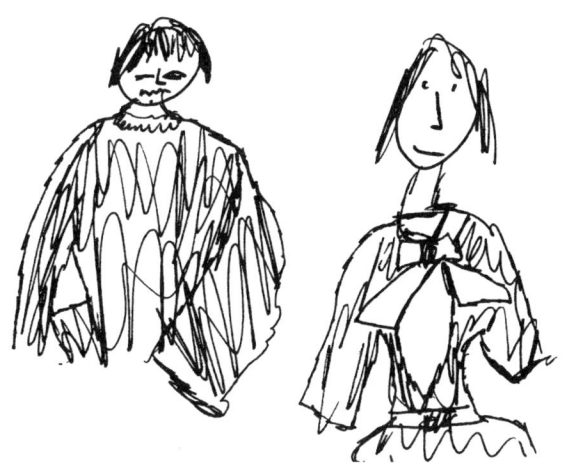

Oscar Rejlander
*Two Ways of Life.*
Albumen print from copy negative of composite photograph, 1857

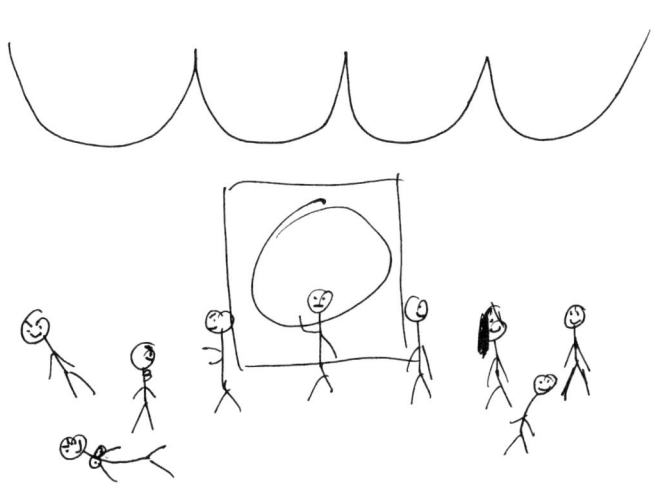

Henry Peach Robinson
*Bringing Home the May.*
Albumen print from copy negative of composite photograph, 1862

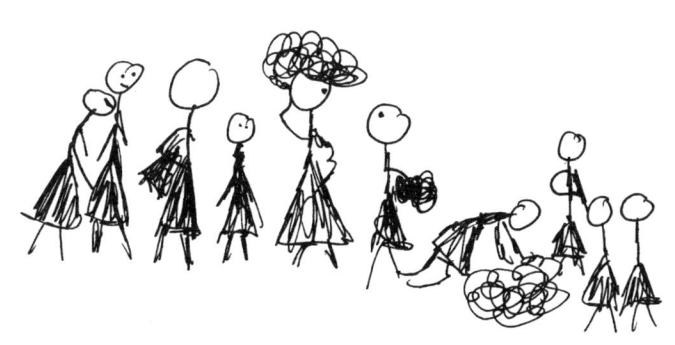

Alexander Gardner
*Execution of Lincoln Assassination Conspirators.*
Albumen print from wet-plate negative, 1865

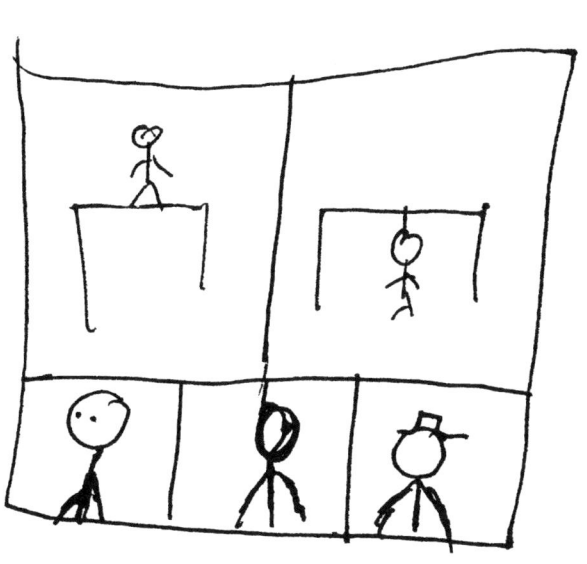

Anonymous (possibly Andre Disderi)
*Communards in Their Coffins.*
Albumen print from wet-plate negative, 1871

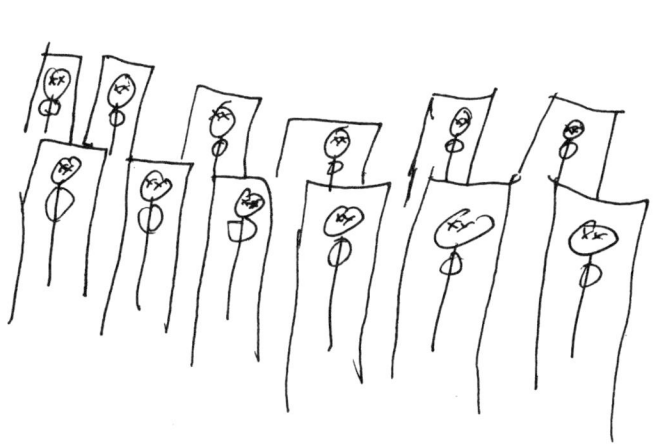

Pierre-Louis Pierson
*Vengeance.*
Albumen print from wet-plate negative, 1863-67

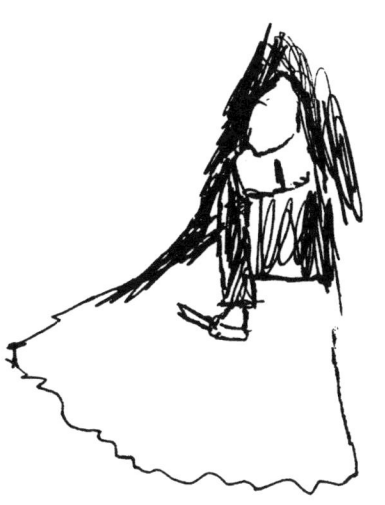

Julia Margaret Cameron
*Ophelia.*
Albumen print from wet-plate negative, 1867

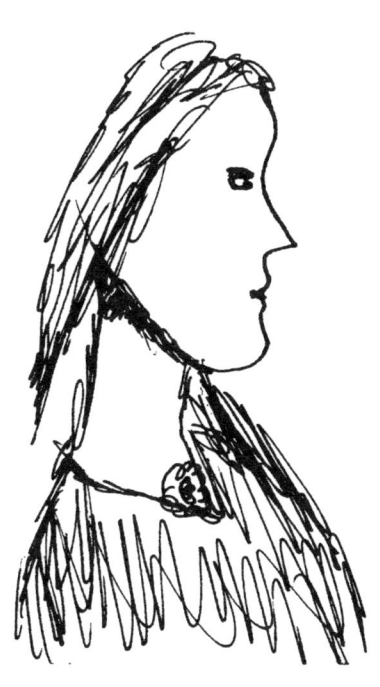

Kusakabe Kimbei
*Girl in a Heavy Storm.*
Albumen print from a wet-plate negative, 1880

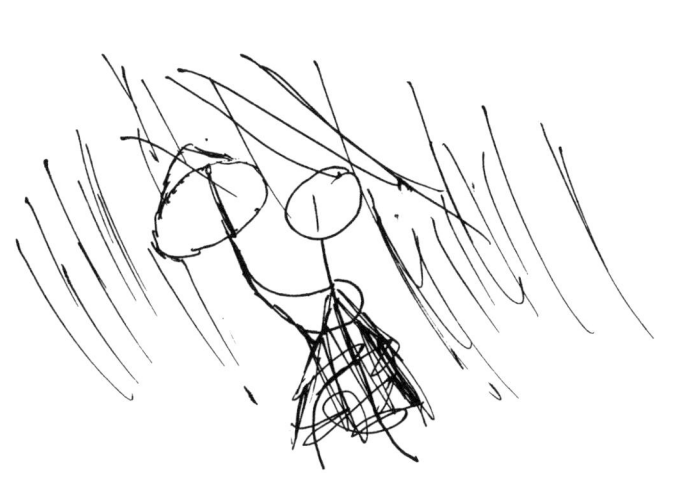

Eadweard Muybridge
*Lying on a Couch and Turning Over on Side.*
Albumen prints, 1886

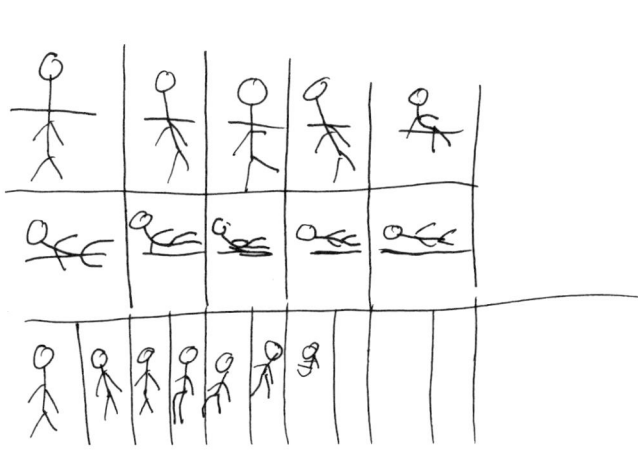

Peter Henry Emerson
*The Clay Mill.*
Platinum print from glass-plate negative, c. 1886 / print c. 1888

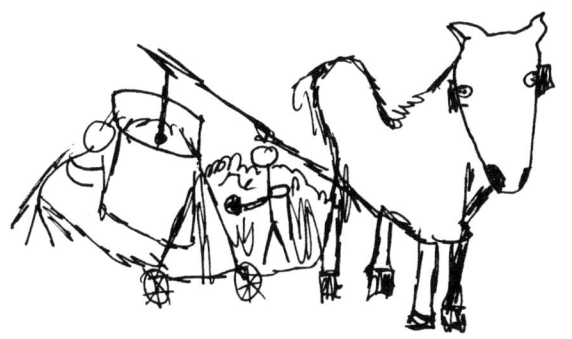

Jacob Riis
*Lodgers in a Crowded Bayard Street Tenement—Five Cents a Spot.*
Gelatin-silver print, 1889

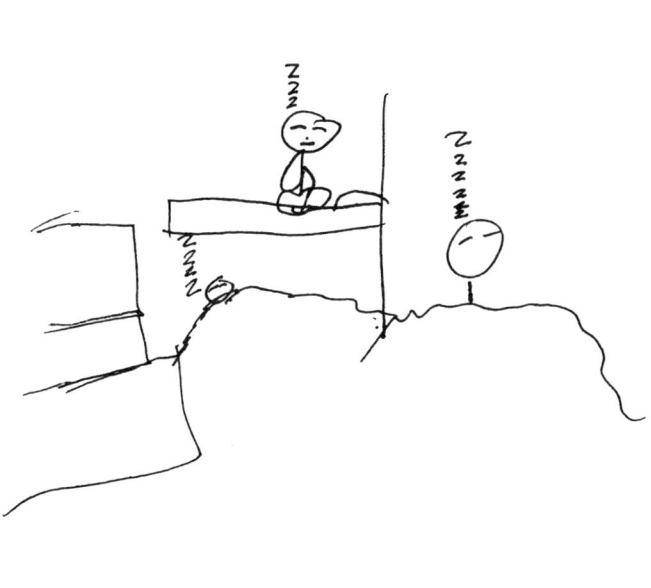

Alfred Stieglitz
*The Steerage.*
Photogravure, 1907

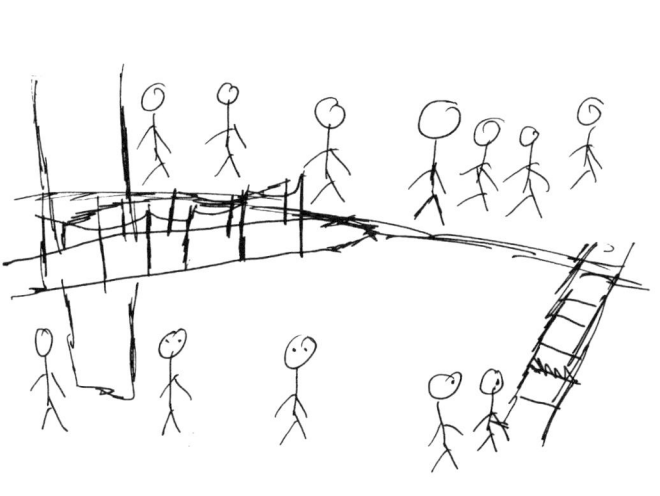

Paul Strand
*Blind Woman.*
Gelatin-silver print from glass-plate negative, 1916

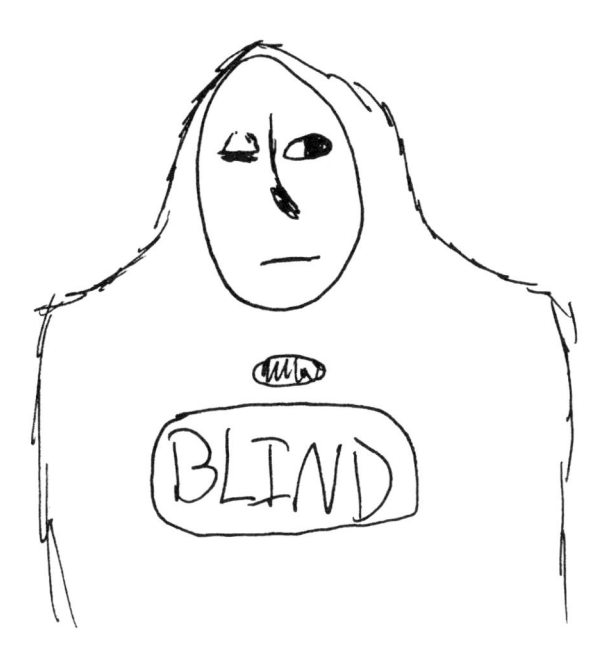

Laszlo Moholy-Nagy
*Mask—Self-Portrait.*
Original photogram on gelatin-silver paper, 1922

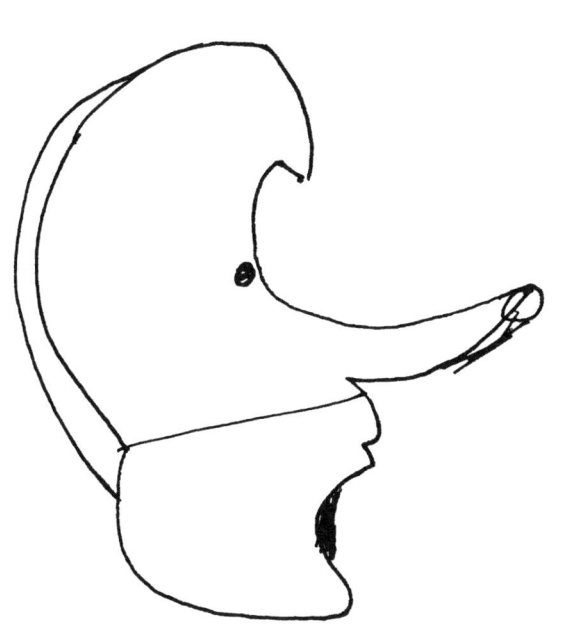

Albert Renger-Patzsch
*Blast Furnace, Herrenwyk.*
Gelatin-silver print from glass-plate negative, 1927

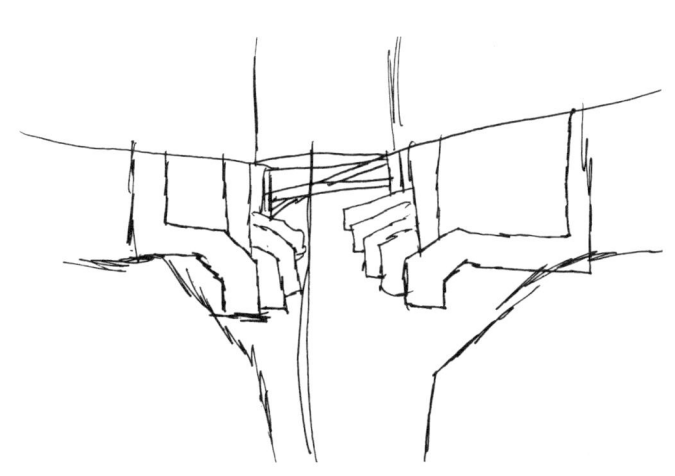

Hannah Hoch
*German Girl*.
Collage from photomechanical reproductions, 1930

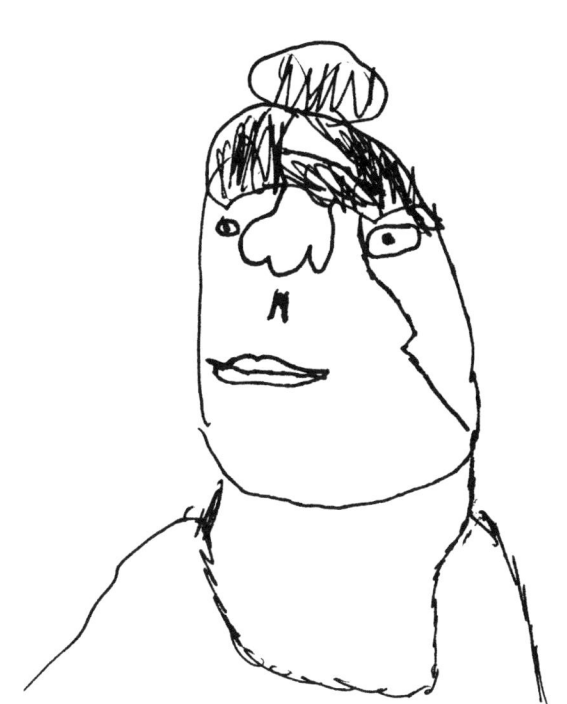

Edward Weston
*Cabbage Leaf.*
Gelatin-silver print from glass-plate negative, 1931

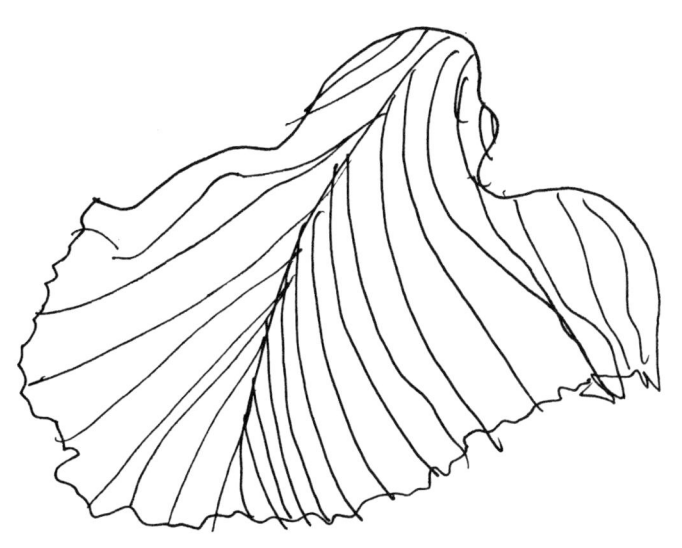

August Sander
*Pastry Cook / Varnisher.*
Gelatin-silver prints, 1928 / 1932

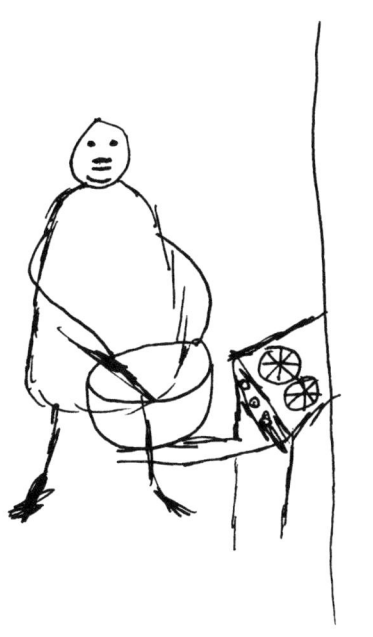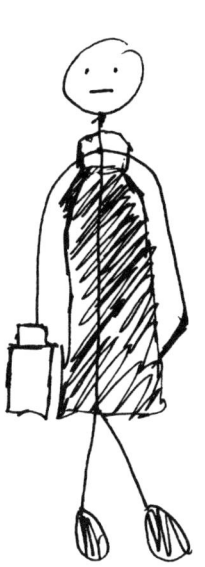

Henri Cartier-Bresson
*Behind the Gare St. Lazare, Paris.*
Gelatin-silver print, 1932

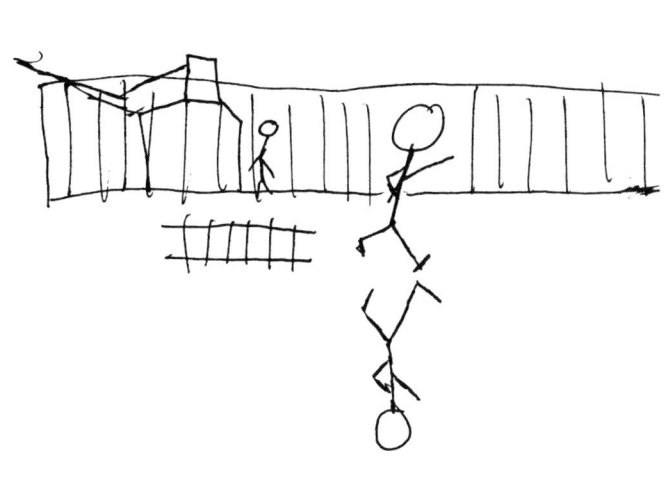

Alexander Rodchenko
*Concert During a Work Break.*
Gelatin-silver print, 1933

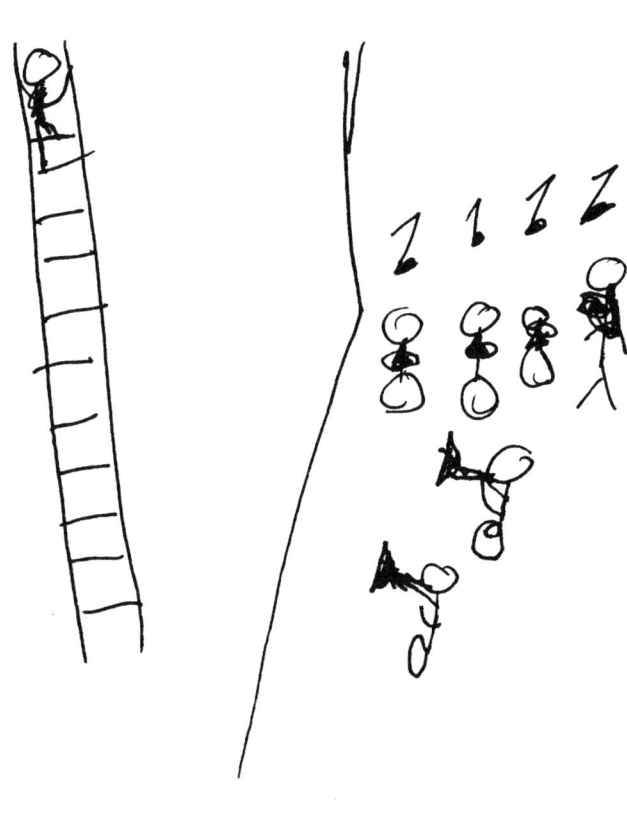

John Heartfield
*Hurrah, the Butter is all Gone!*
Photomontage, 1935

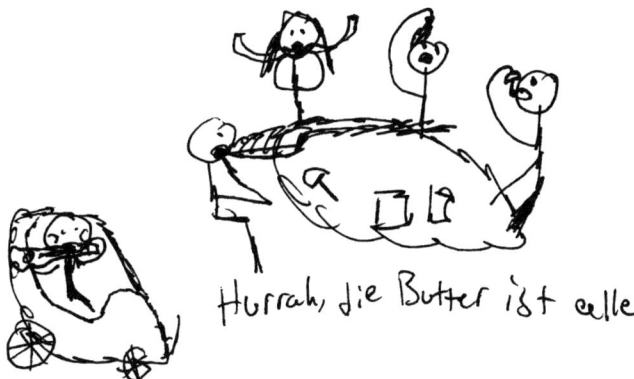

Dorothea Lange
*Family, Texas.*
Gelatin-silver print, 1936

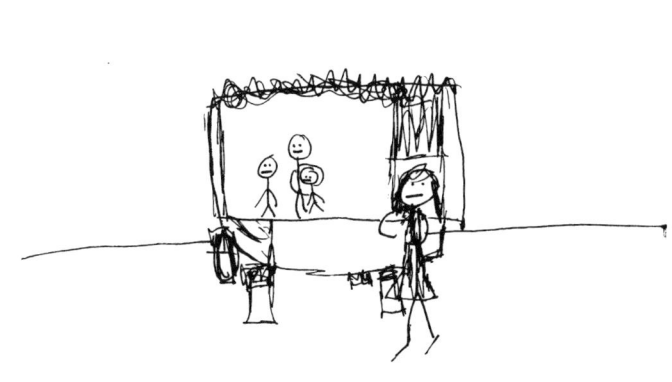

Walker Evans
*Bed, Tenant Farmhouse, Hale County Alabama.* Gelatin-silver print, 1935
From *Let Us Now Praise Famous Men*, 1939

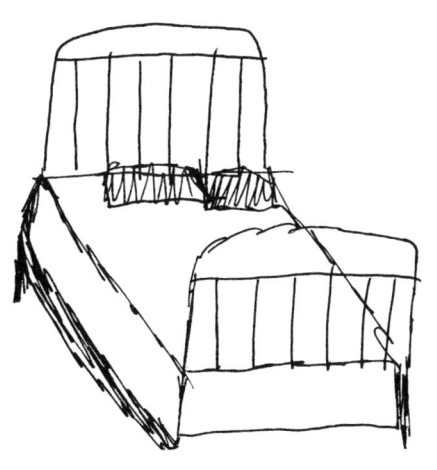
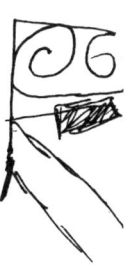

Robert Capa
*Normandy.*
Gelatin-silver print, 1944

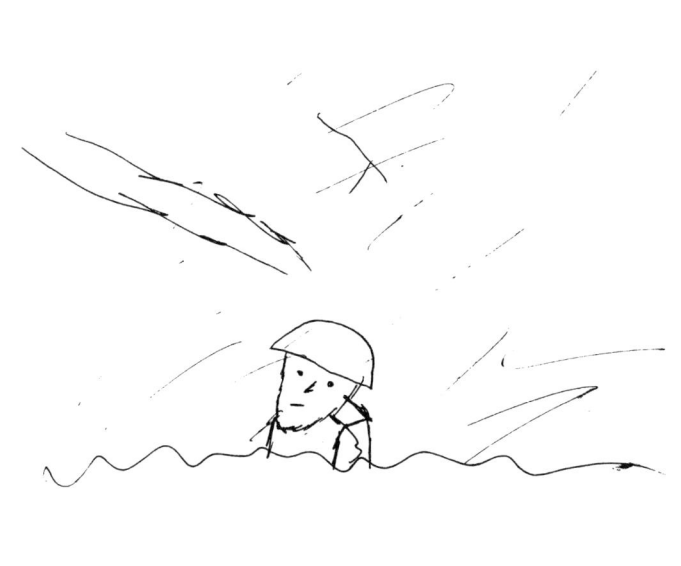

W. Eugene Smith
*Country Doctor.*
Gelatin-silver print, 1948

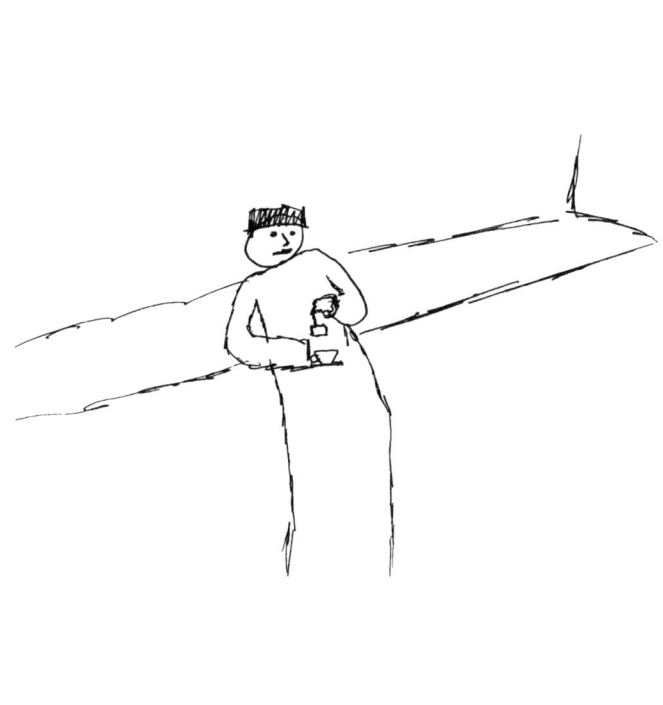

Robert Frank
*Parade, Hoboken, NJ.* Gelatin-silver print, 1955/56
From *The Americans,* 1958

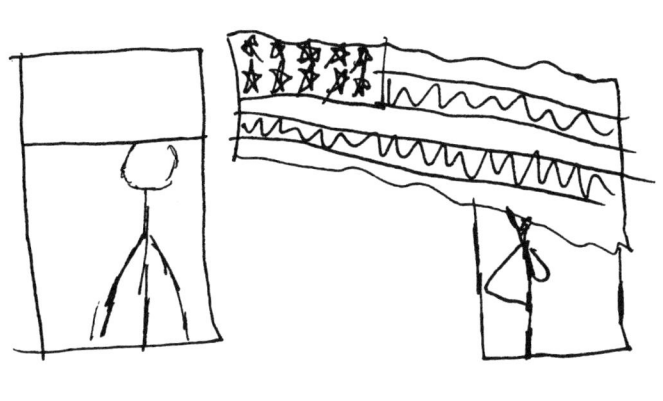

Garry Winogrand
*San Francisco.*
Gelatin-silver print, 1964

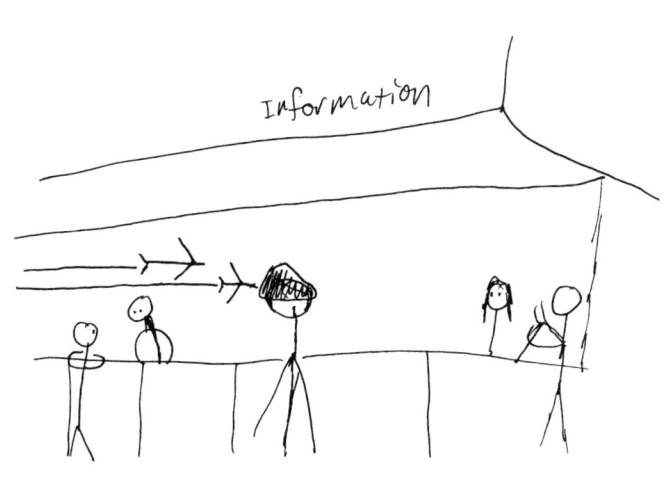

Ed Ruscha
*Hollywood Bowl* (from *Thirty-four Parking Lots*).
1967

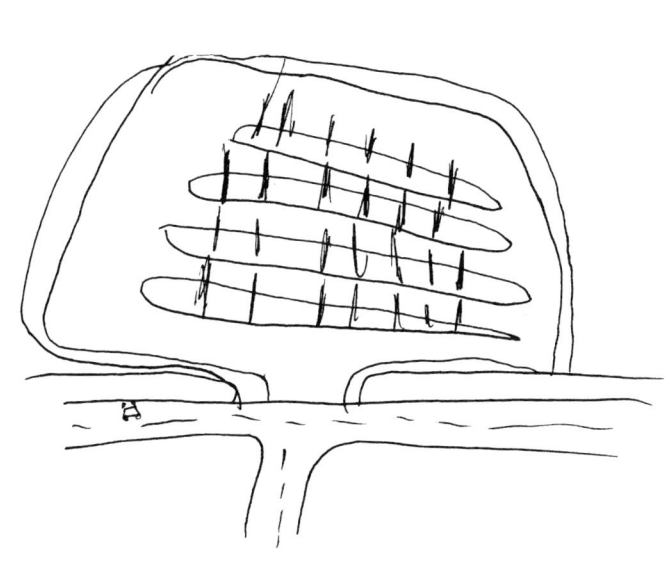

Diane Arbus
*Topless Dancer in her Dressing Room.*
Gelatin-silver print, 1968

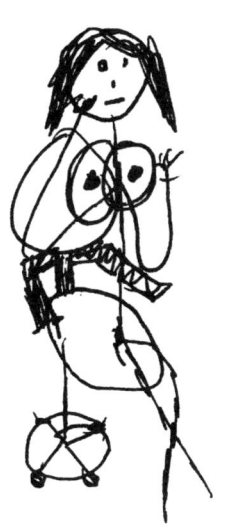

Robert Mapplethorpe
*Mark Stevens (Mr. 10 1/2).*
Gelatin-silver print, 1976

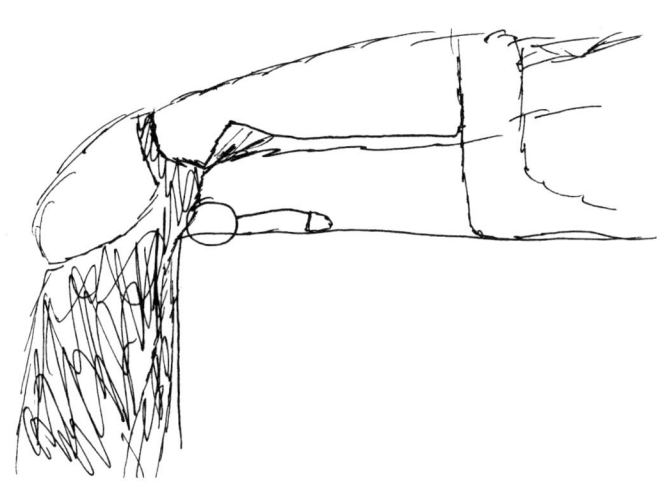

William Eggleston
*Sumner, Mississippi, Cassidy Bayou in Background.* Dye-transfer print, c. 1970
From *William Eggleston's Guide*, 1976

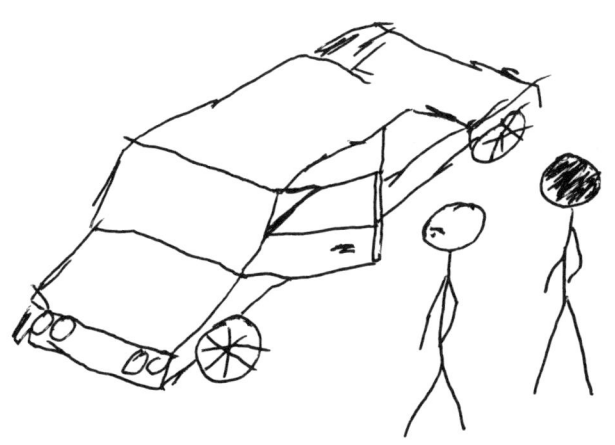

Cindy Sherman
From *Untitled Film Stills.*
Gelatin-silver print, 1977-80

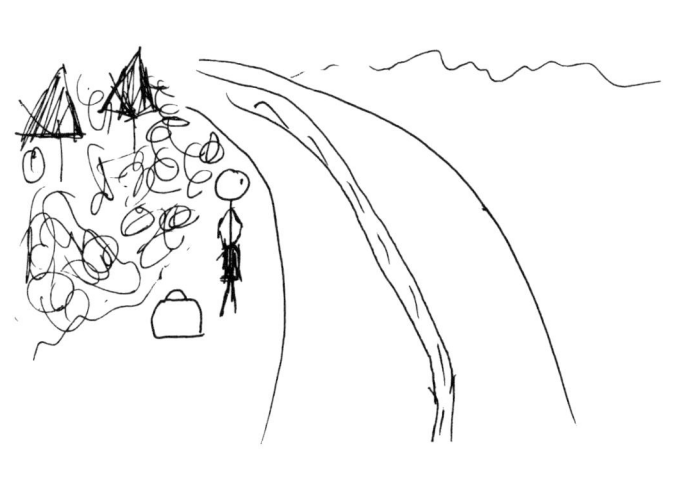

Nan Goldin
*Trixie on the Cot, New York City.*
Dye-destruction print, 1979

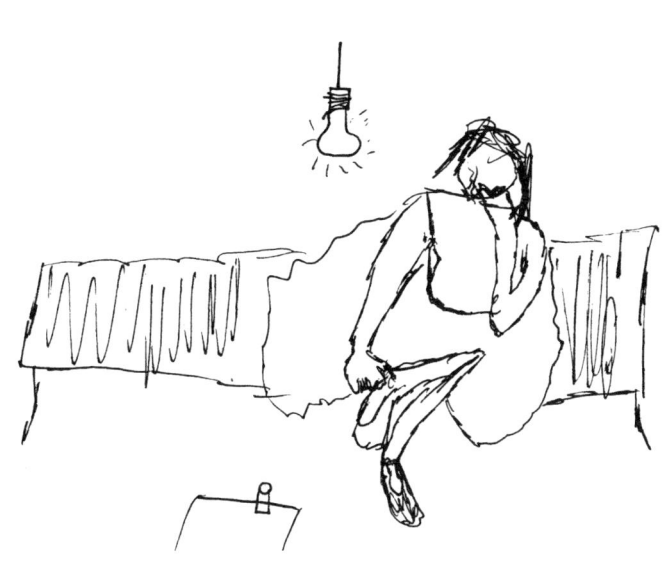

Joel Sternfeld
*Wet 'n Wild Aquatic Theme Park.*
Chromogenic development print, 1980

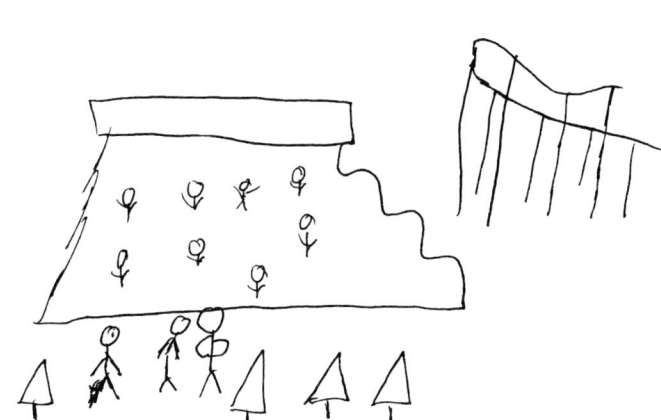

Bernd & Hilla Becher
*Blast Furnace Heads.*
Gelatin-silver prints, 1988

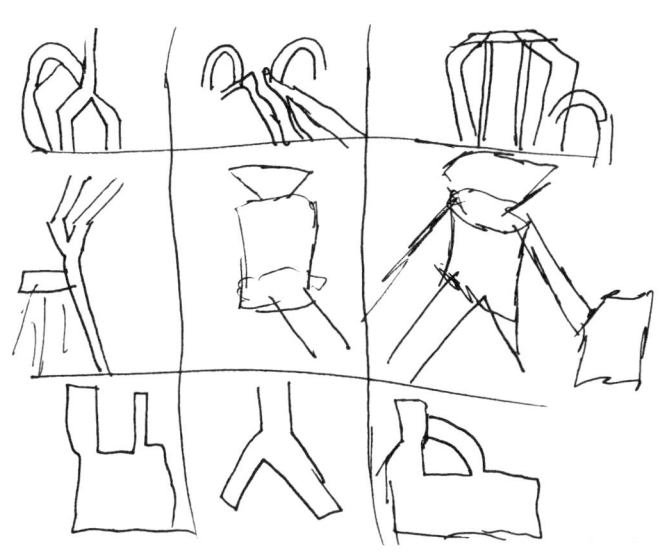

Thomas Struth
*Art Institute of Chicago II.*
Chromogenic development print, 1990

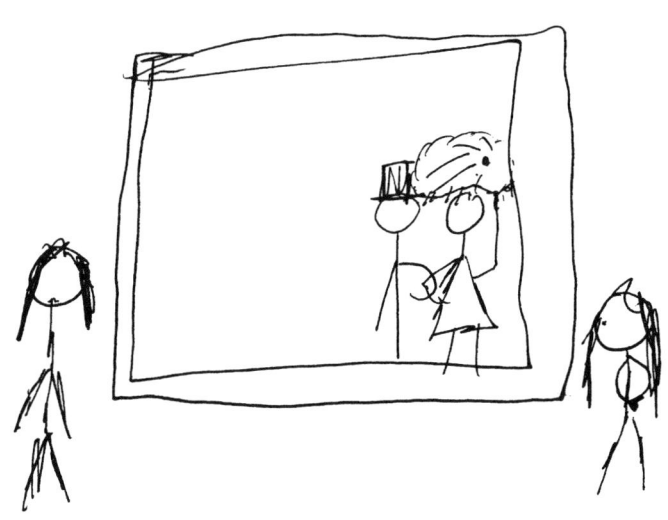

THE HISTORY OF PHOTOGRAPHY IN PEN & INK
Second printing
Edition of 1500
© 2009, 2012 Charles Woodard and A-Jump Books
Illustrations by Charles Woodard
Book design by A-Jump Studios
Printed in Hong Kong

ISBN: 978-0-9777655-9-1

*...photography grasps what is given as a spatial (or temporal) continuum; memory images retain what is given only insofar as it has significance.*

— Siegfried Kracauer, PHOTOGRAPHY

A-Jump Books, Ithaca, NY
www.a-jumpbooks.com
info@a-jumpbooks.com